GRADE 2 SOCIAL SCIENCE

Fun-filled Activities

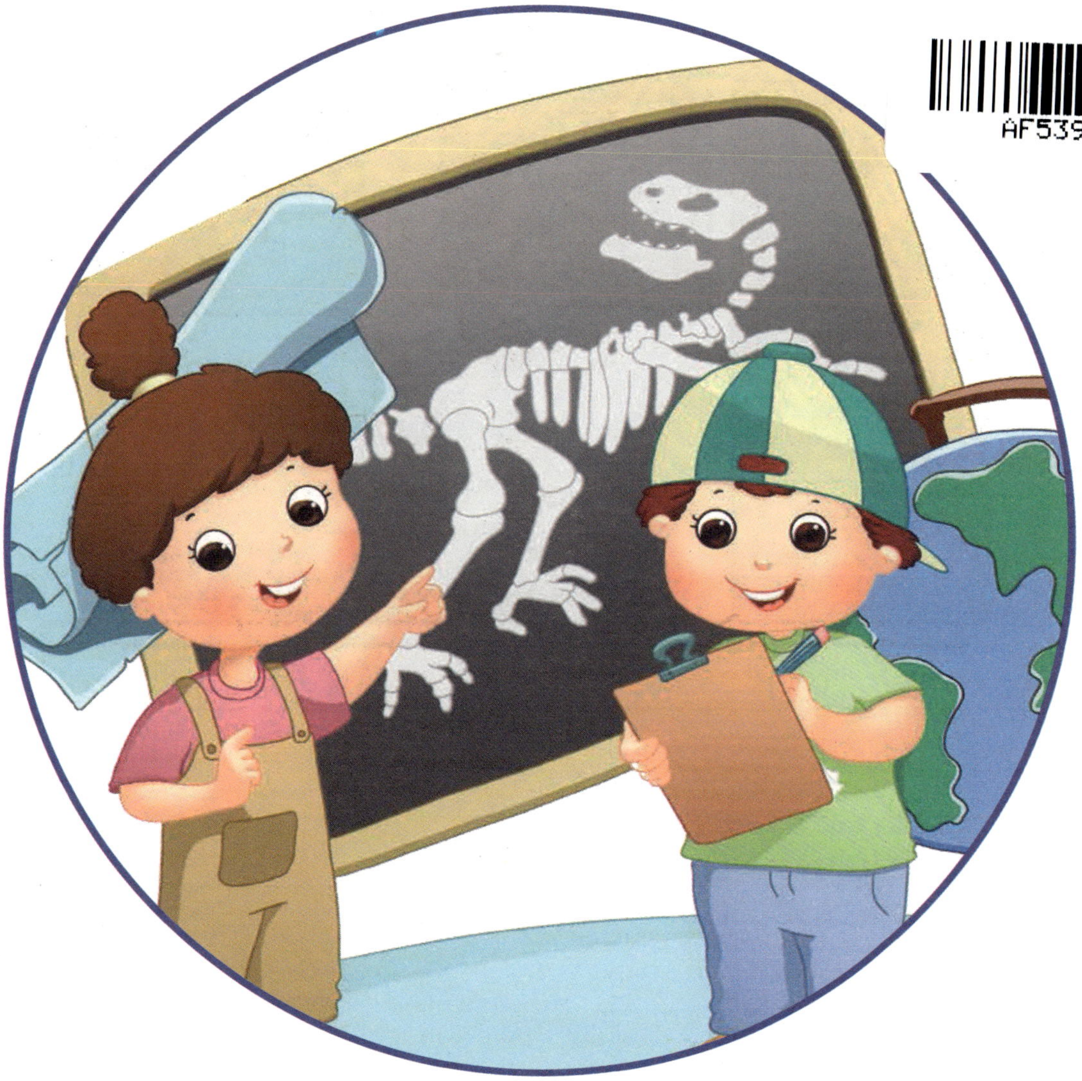

Om KIDZ
An imprint of Om Books International

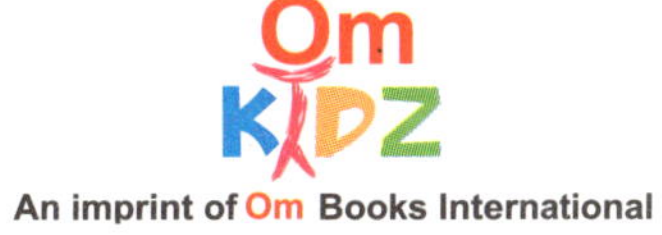

Family

A family is a unit of parents and their children living together.

Look at the pictures and write what families do together.

Draw your family doing something together.

Family

This is Jack's family. Use these words to label the picture.

father, mother, grandfather, grandmother, brother, sister

Write if these statements are true or false.

1. James is Jack's grandfather. ________
2. Linda is Alice's daughter. ________
3. Neo is James's father. ________
4. Jack is Doris's grandson. ________
5. Alice is James's wife. ________
6. Doris is Linda's grandmother. ________
7. James is Linda's father. ________
8. Jack is Alice's son. ________

Our Needs and Wants

Needs are things without which it would be difficult to live or survive.

Wants are things we would like to have but don't need to live.

Draw a line from the word to the picture it goes with.

1. need
2. want

3. need
4. want

5. need
6. want

7. need
8. want

We Live in a Neighbourhood

Look at the drawing of Nancy's neighbourhood and fill in the blanks.

A neighbourhood is a place where people live. Every neighbourhood has homes, school, shops and other places.

Sterling Apartments
Park
Bus stop
Grocery store
Cleaner's shop
Hardware shop
Dau Cleaners

1. Nancy's neighbourhood has a ________________, __________________, park, ________________ and ________________.
2. Nancy lives in __________________________.
3. ______________ is to the left of Nancy's apartments.
4. Nancy and her friends play in the ____________________.
5. Her neighbourhood belongs to a ___________________.

Community

A community is a place where people live and work together for the common good. There are three types of communities – urban, suburban and rural.

- Many people live close together
- Small amount of space
- Less open areas or natural areas
- Tall skyscrapers

- Close to, but not, in cities
- Fewer people
- Small apartments but no Skyscrapers

- Fewer people
- A few buildings spread over large distances
- Lots of open space and natural areas

Try this!

Make a comparison chart to show things that are similar and different in urban, suburban and rural areas.

My Community

Answer these questions about your community.

1. What is the name of your community?____________________
2. Where is it located?________________________________
3. Which large city is it near?____________________________
4. Are there any historical monuments? If so, name them and state where are they located.
   a. ____
   b. ____
5. What is unique about your community?
   a. ____
   b. ____
6. Why do you like your community?
   a. ____
   b. ____

Draw a picture of the community you live in. Write a sentence to describe it.

Goods and Services in a Community

Goods are things that people make or grow.

For example: crops, soap, jute bags

Services are jobs or work that other people do for you.

For example: a barber cuts hair, so he provides us a service.

Goods
apples for sale

Service
a barber cutting hair

Write goods or services for the pictures given below..

______________ ______________ ______________

______________ ______________ ______________

Help!

There are many community services that help you in different ways. Which one should you call for each problem below?

Draw a line to match the need with the place that meets it.

1. You need help finding a fact for your science homework.
2. You see a fire out of your window.
3. You find a lost bag on the street.
4. You want to use the park for your cricket team party.
5. Someone has been hurt.
6. You need to find a zip code.
7. You see a leaking water pipe in your locality.
8. The garbage in your neighbourhood has not been picked up for 3 days.
9. There is a dangerous dog straying in your neighbourhood.
10. The electricity has gone out on your street.

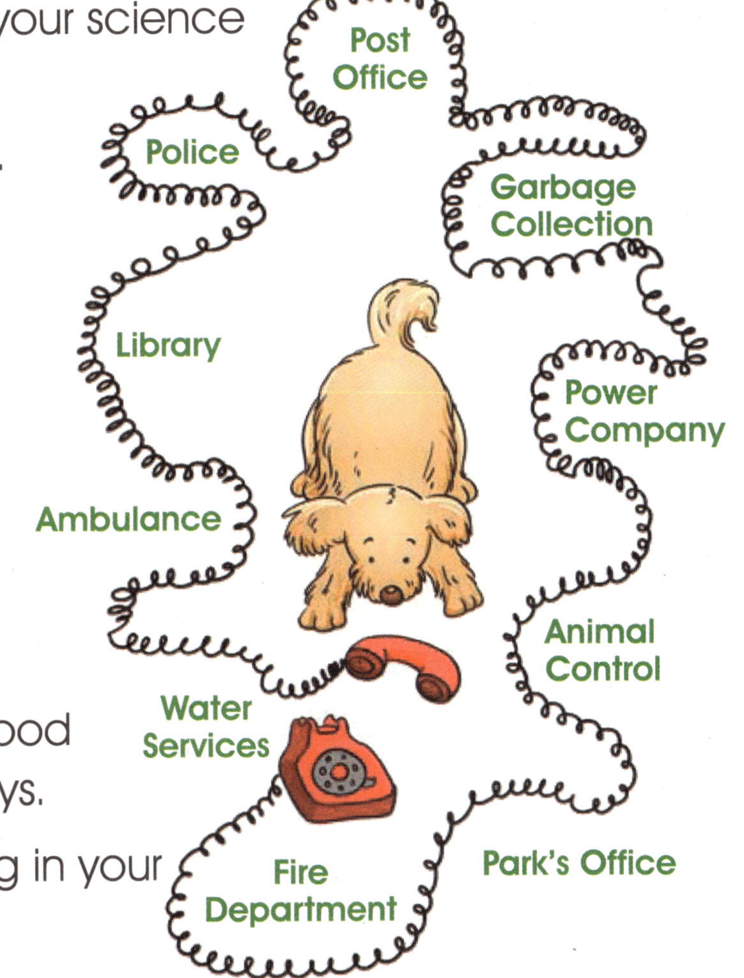

Try this!

It is Saturday and Norman has a lot to do today. He has to go to the library to find a book about transport. Then he has to go to the clinic to get medicine for Granny. Next, he has to buy some postage stamps for his Mom. Lastly, for his Dad, he has to find out what time the soccer game starts. Name all services Norman would use.

Rules in a Community

Just as we have rules in the family, we need to follow certain rules and laws in our community to keep ourselves safe and peaceful.

Write agree or disagree for these rules in the community.

1. No talking in the library.

2. No driving while operating a mobile phone.

3. All owners of television sets must have a licence.

4. No littering in shopping malls.

5. Spitting chewing gum in public places.

6. Walk on the track in a park.

7. Ignore traffic signals if you are in a hurry.

8. No seat belts while driving.

9. Playing loud music in the neighbourhood.

10. Park your car anywhere in the market.

Think about it

You are walking around the supermarket and are very hungry so you pick up a bar of chocolate; you eat it and throw away the wrapper before you exit. Is this OK?

Rules in a Community

Look at the picture and talk to your friend about it.

1. Who has broken a rule in this picture?

____

2. What has the driver of the yellow car done that is wrong?

____

3. What do you think the traffic police officer should do?

____

Think about it

What should you do when you see someone breaking a rule in the school?

Community Signs and Symbols

We see different signs and symbols around us. These signs and symbols keep us safe and also aware of the community.

Look at these signs and symbols. Write the name of each sign. Choose from the help box.

______

______

______

______

______

______

______

______

______

______

______

______

______

______

______

Help Box

Railroad crossing	Stop	Bike Route	Caution
Handicapped	No Pedestrian	Phone	No Bike
School crossing	Men	Women	Exit
Bus stop	Hospital	Emergency	Walk

People Communicate

Communication means sending information from one person to another. Talking is the most common way of communicating that we all know.

We can also communicate by other ways such as:

writing letters

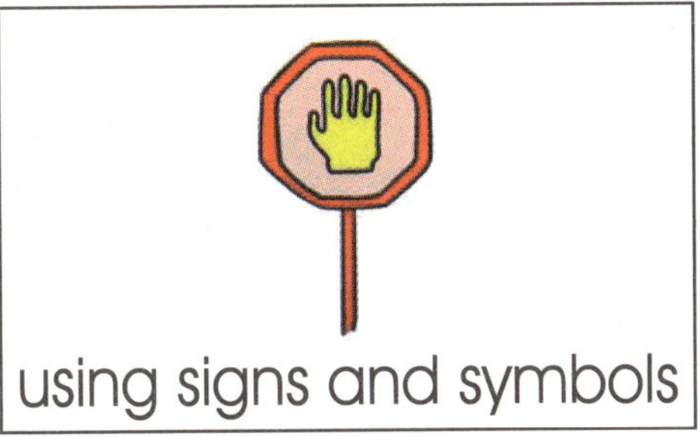
using signs and symbols

email

newspapers

books

postcard

telephone

radio

television

fax

music

advertisements

Think about it

Look at these words and sentences. We can tell someone all these things without talking. Take turns with your friend to show how we communicate each one.

1. Come here 2. No 3. Quiet 4. I am angry 5. Stop

People Communicate

Look at the picture. How many different ways of communication can you find?

1. How many people are reading something?

____

2. What kind of reading can we do for fun?

____

3. What do we read every day to find what is happening in our city and country?

____

4. What kind of communication is the "wet paint"?

____

5. Name one warning sign you see in the picture.

____

People Communicate

Tick the correct option in each sentence.

1. We get stamps from the **(newspaper office/post office).**
2. **(Letters/ e-mails)** are sent through internet.
3. **(Telephone/Television)** is the fastest means of communication.
4. We can carry **(telephones/mobile phones)** with us.
5. A **(letter/television)** is a means of mass communication.
6. You can find lots of information on any subject in a **(postcard/book).**
7. A **(e-mail/newspaper)** is a printed means of communication.

Pretend you are on holiday in a town that you have not been to before.

Write a postcard to your friend about everything you have seen and done.

Using Transportation

We use different kinds of transport to get from one place to another and to move things from one place to another. There are many different kinds of transport. Most of us travel by land on roads, trains and footpaths. We also use roads and trains to transport things by land.

In each sentence below, cross the information that is wrong. Correct the sentences and rewrite them.

1. Thousands of years ago, man used to travel from one place to another using a car.

   ____

2. In rural areas, people usually travel by bullet trains.

   ____

3. Dogs were used to pull carts some years ago.

   ____

4. Things like coal, vehicles and goods are transported by passenger trains.

   ____

5. The fastest means of transportation is train.

   ____

6. A yacht is a ship that remains inside the water.

   ____

7. Trains run on steel tracks that are called cars.

   ____

8. A helicopter can carry large number of people.

   ____

Mapping my Neighbourhood

A map is a drawing of a place. Maps can be drawn to represent a variety of information such as roads, directions, places and more.

A map has:

Big Island

a title

name given to the map

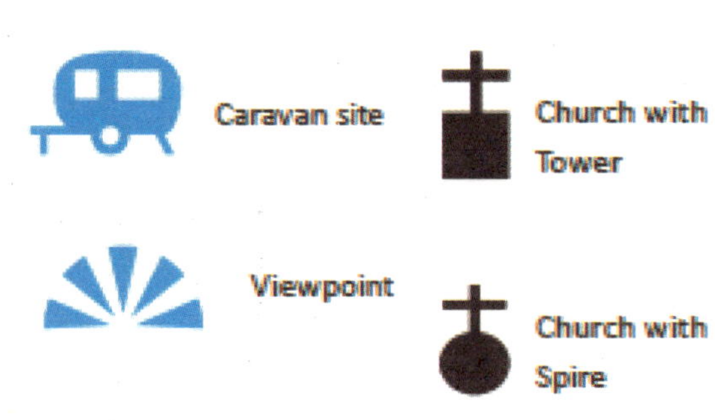

symbols

can be line, shape or colour

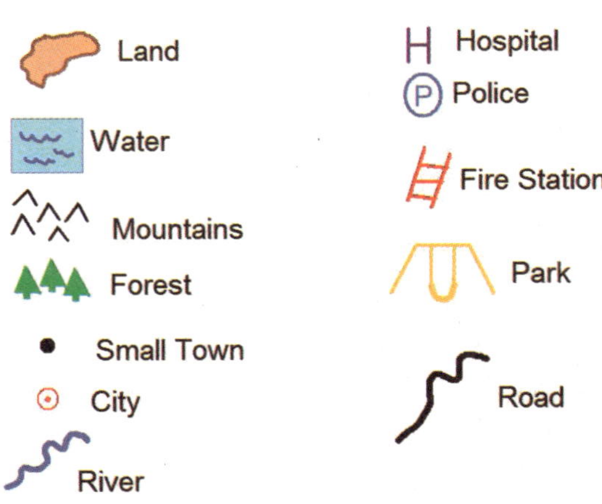

legend or key

tell what the symbols mean

compass rose

shows direction on a map

Pictures and Maps

The model below shows Kate's community from an aeroplane. Study it and answer the questions.

Kate's Community

Circle the map that shows Kate's community..

Map A

Map B

Try this!

Look for pictures that show a community in an aerial view, Can you identify houses and other places in the community?

Pictures and Maps

Polly and her friends are playing hide and seek. Help her find her friends by looking at the map. Answer the questions.

1. Where is Alice hiding? ___________________________
2. Who is in the dining room? ___________________________
3. Who is hiding in the room next to Mom's room? ___________________
4. Where is Polly's room? Circle it. ___________________________
5. How many rooms does Polly's house have? _______________________

Finding Directions on a Map

Look at the picture and answer the questions.

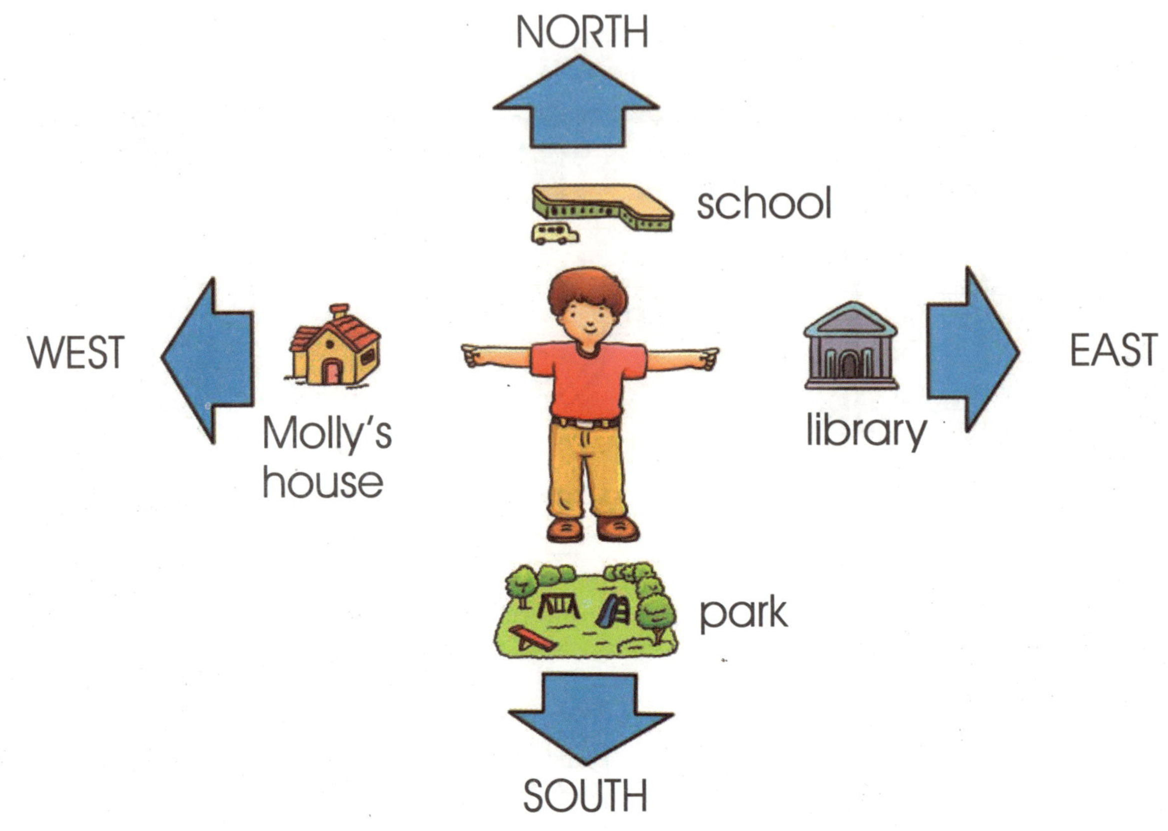

1. Name the four directions you see on the map.

   ____

2. In which direction should Daniel walk to go to school?

   ____

3. In which direction is the library?

   ____

4. Daniel wants to go to the park. In which direction should he move?

   ____

5. Molly's house is to the ______________ of Daniel.

Try this!

Stand in front of your house facing the north. Name the places that are to your east, west and south.

Map of the Zoo

Look at the map of the zoo. Then answer the questions.

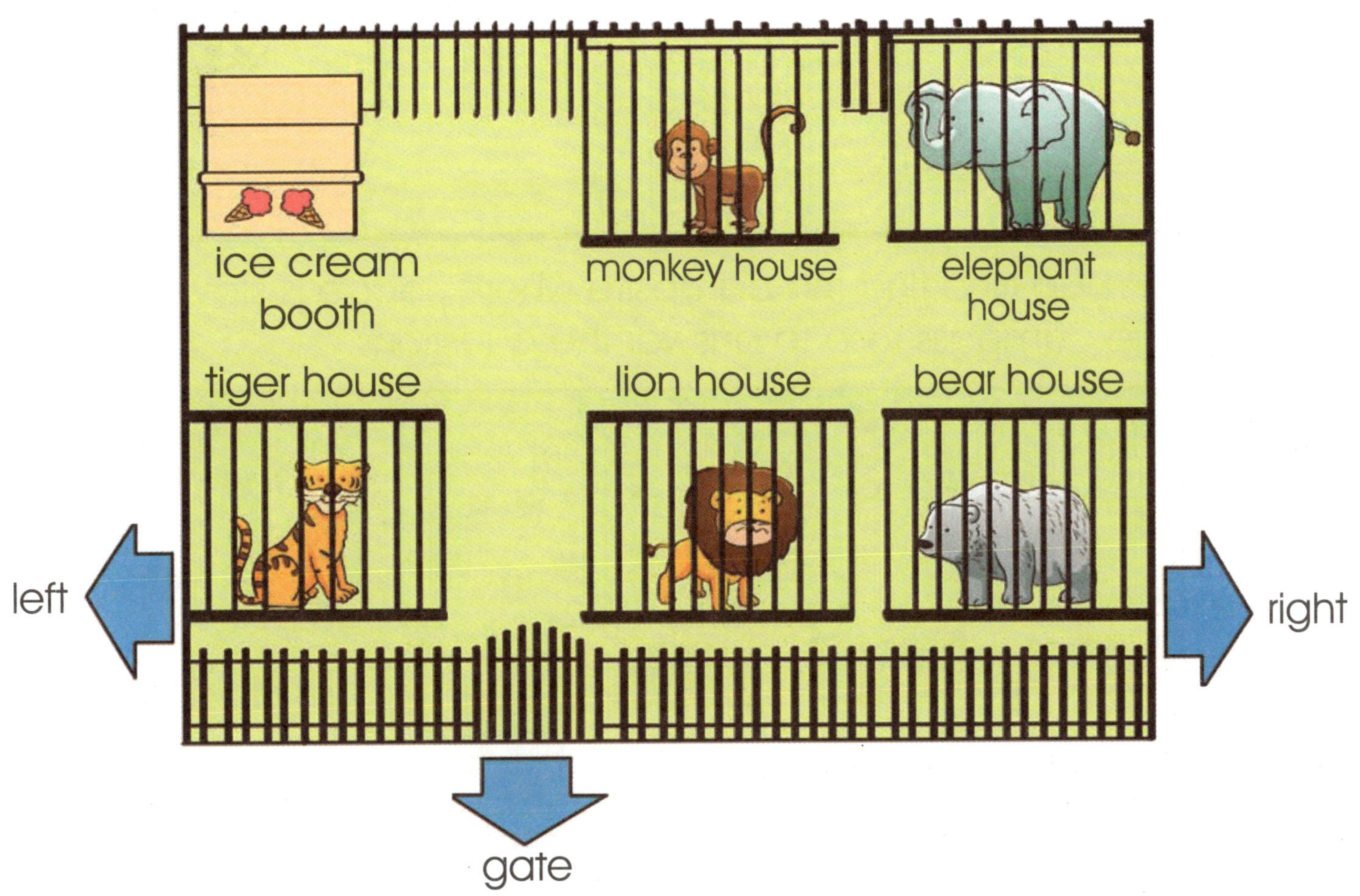

1. Which house is to the right of the ice cream booth?

____

2. Which house is to the left of lion's house?

____

3. Which house is to the right of monkey's house?

____

4. How many houses are to the right of tiger's house?

____

5. If you stand where the bear is, which house would be to your right and left?

____

Using a Compass Rose

A compass rose is a figure on a compass, map, chart or monument used to show directions: North, East, South and West.

Compass rose

Look at the map and find the campsite where Jacob is staying. Then use the compass rose to answer the questions.

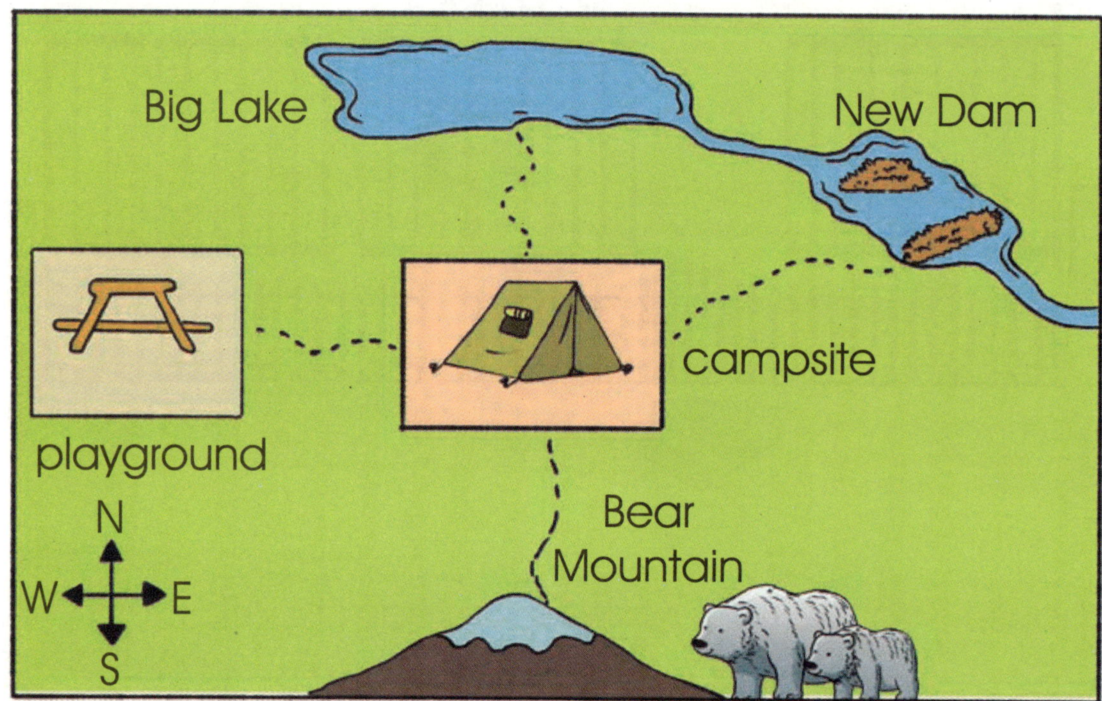

1. In which direction should Jacob walk to reach the playground?

____

2. Is the Bear Mountain to the west or south of the campsite?

____

3. In which direction should Jacob walk to reach the Big Lake?

____

4. Is the New Dam east or west of the Big Lake?

____

Using Map Symbols

Look at the map of a community below. Use the map and map symbols to answer the questions.

1. There are many houses in the community. Which symbol stands for a house?

2. What is to the east of the park? Circle it on the map.

____

3. What is the symbol of the community centre? Draw it here.

____

4. How many schools do you see on the map? Put a (✓) on the map.

____

5. Which symbol shows the playground?

Try this!

Draw a line to show the route you can take to reach the school from the community centre. Which directions you moved in?

Using a Map Key

A map key helps to study the information needed for the map to make sense. It explains what symbols or colours on a map mean.

Look at the map key. Find the symbols and circle them. Then answer the questions.

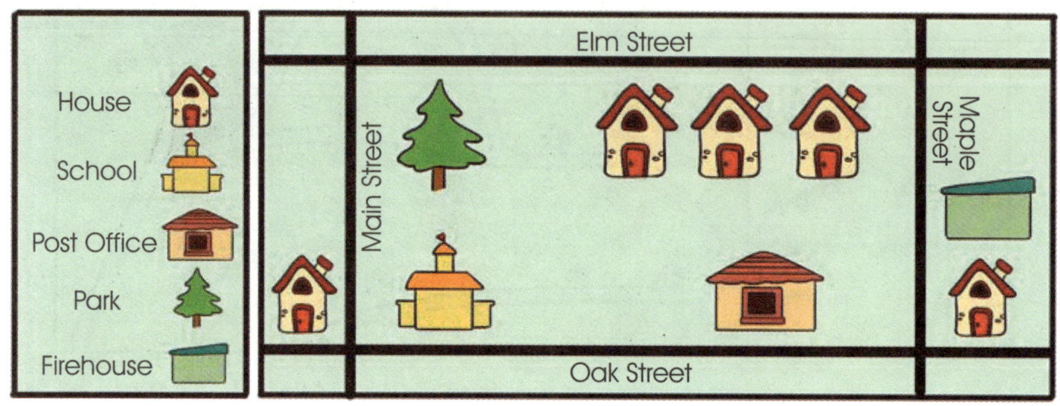

1. Which symbol stands for the park?

2. Which symbol stands for the firehouse?

3. How many houses can you see on the map?

____

4. Name the streets on the map.

____

5. Find the post office on the map and circle it.

Try this! Make a map showing any 5 places around your neighbourhood. Use your own symbols and key.

Studying a Map

Look at the map carefully. Then answer the questions.

1. Which seas are to the west of England?

____

2. In which direction is Scotland from England?

____

3. In which direction should you move from Ireland to go to England?

____

4. Draw the symbols that show the mountains and river.

____

5. How many rivers do you see on the map? Name them.

____

Landforms and Water

A landform is a natural feature of the Earth's surface.

Try this!

How are a mountain, a hill and a valley different from one another?

Landforms and Water

Look at the drawing of different landforms and write the word used to describe:

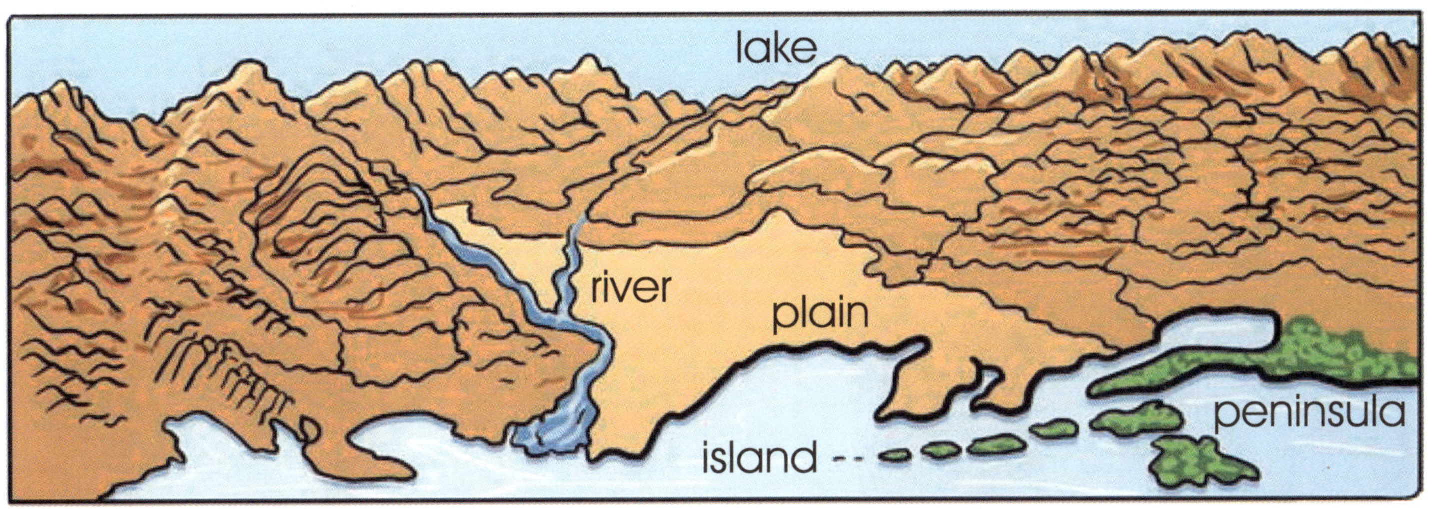

1. An area of land with water all around it.

____

2. A water body with land all around it.

____

3. A flat land.

____

4. A large natural stream of water flowing in a channel to the sea.

____

5. An area of land surrounded by water on three sides.

____

Try this!

Use your own words to define: a desert, a pond, a coast

Natural Resources

Natural resources are materials or substances occurring in nature which can be used by us.

For example: land, water, soil, sunlight

Look at the pictures. Put a tick on the natural resources.

Taking Care of Natural Resources

Tick the picture that shows ways to care for natural resources.

Throw litter on the ground

Throw litter in the trash can

Use things again

Take care of birds and animals

Help to keep the surroundings clean

Answer Key

Page 2

play

celebrate festivals

read and study

go on a picnic

Page 3

1. False
2. True
3. True
4. True
5. True
6. True
7. True
8. true

Page 4

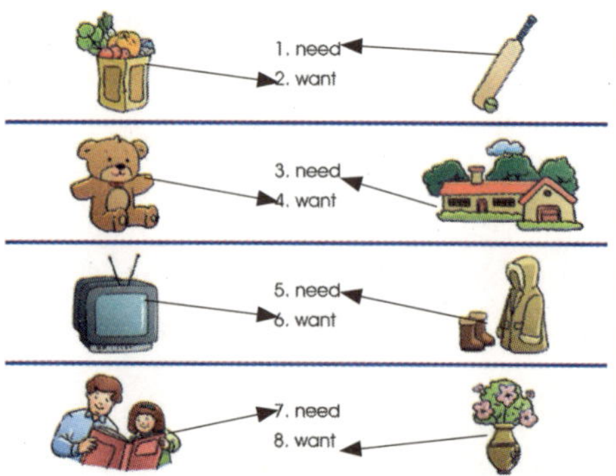

Page 5

1. cleaner's shop, grocery store, bus stop, hardware shop
2. Sterling Apartments
3. France Groceries
4. park
5. city

Page 7

Children will do on their own.
Answers will vary.

Page 8

Page 9

1. Library
2. Fire Department
3. Police
4. Park's Office
5. Ambulance
6. Post Office
7. Water Services
8. Garbage Collection
9. Animal Control
10. Power Company

Page 10

1. agree
2. agree
3. disagree
4. agree
5. disagree
6 agree
7. disagree
8. disagree
9. disagree
10. disagree

Page 11

1. The driver of the yellow car.
2. The driver of the yellow car has skipped the red light.
3. The policeman should stop and warn him for breaking rules.

Answer Key

Page 12

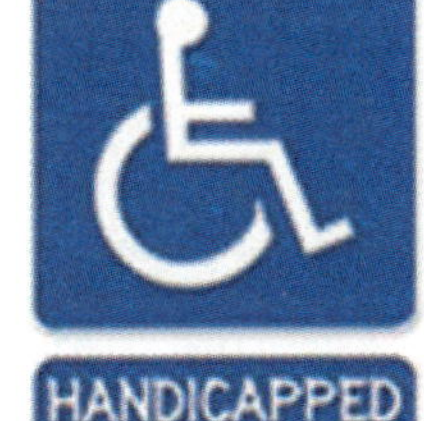

Page 14

1. One
2. Read books
3. Newspaper
4. Sign board
5. Danger! No swimming

Page 15

1. Post office
2. E-mails
3. Telephone
4. Mobile phones
5. Television
6. Book
7. Newspaper

Page 16

1. False- Thousands of years ago, man used to travel from one place to another using carts, animals.
2. False- In rural areas, people usually travel by carts, other small vehicles.
3. False- Horses were used to pull carts some years ago
4. False- Things like coal, vehicles and goods are transported by goods trains.
5. False- The fastest means of transportation is aeroplane.
6. False- A submarine remains inside the water.
7. False- Trains run on steel tracks that are called tracks.
8. False- A helicopter can carry less number of people.

Page 18

Map A is Kate's neighbourhood.

Page 19

1. Mom's room
2. Ron
3. Kim
4. Children will circle on their own.
5. Seven

Page 20

1. North, south, east, west
2. North
3. East
4. South
5. West

Page 21

1. Monkey house
2. Tiger house
3. Elephant house
4. Two
5. Lion house would be to the left and no house on the right

Page 22

1. West
2. South
3. North
4. East

Answer Key

Page 23

1. 

2. A house

3. 

4. One

Page 24

1. 

2. 

3. five
4. Elm Street, Main Street, Oak Street, Maple Street
5. Children will circle the post office on their own

Page 25

1. Irish Sea, Celtic Sea
2. North
3. East
4. Children will draw symbols on their own.
5. There are three rivers.

Page 27

1. Island
2. Lake
3. Plain
4. River
5. peninsula

Page 28

water, fruits, soil, wool and wood are natural resources

Page 29

These are ways to take care of natural resources:

- Throw litter in the trash can
- Use things again
- Take care of birds and animals
- Help to keep the surroundings clean